IMAGES
of America

HUDSON'S NATIONAL GUARD MILITIA

I Am The Guard

Civilian in Peace, Soldier in War... of security and honor, for three centuries I have been the custodian, I am the Guard.

I was with Washington in the dim forests, fought the wily warrior, and watched the dark night bow to the morning. At Concord's bridge, I fired the fateful shot heard 'round the world. I bled on Bunker Hill. My footprints marked the snows at Valley Forge. I pulled a muffled oar on the barge that bridged the icy Delaware. I stood with Washington on the sun-drenched heights of Yorktown. I saw the sword surrendered... I am the Guard. I pulled the trigger that loosed the long rifle's havoc at New Orleans. These things I knew--I was there! I saw both sides of the War between the States--I was there! The hill at San Juan felt the fury of my charge. The far plains and mountains of the Philippines echoed to my shout... On the Mexican border I stood... I am the Guard. The dark forest of the Argonne blazed with my barrage. Chateau Thierry crumbled to my cannonade. Under the arches of victory I marched in legion -- I was there! I am the Guard. I bowed briefly on the grim Corregidor, then saw the light of liberation shine on the faces of my comrades. Through the jungle and on the beaches, I fought the enemy, beat, battered and broke him. I raised our banner to the serene air on Okinawa--I scrambled over Normandy's beaches--I was there!... I am the Guard. Across the 38th Parallel I made my stand. I flew MiG Alley. I was there!... I am the Guard.

Soldier in war, civilian in peace... I am the Guard.

I was at Johnstown, where the raging waters boomed down the valley. I cradled the crying child in my arms and saw the terror leave her eyes. I moved through smoke and flame at Texas City. The stricken knew the comfort of my skill. I dropped the food that fed the starving beast on the frozen fields of the west and through the towering drifts I ploughed to rescue the marooned. I have faced forward to the tornado, the typhoon, and the horror of the hurricane and flood... these things I know -- I was there! I am the Guard. I have brought a more abundant, a fuller, a finer life to our youth. Wherever a strong arm and valiant spirit must defend the Nation, in peace or war, wherever a child cries, or a woman weeps in time of disaster, there I stand... I am the Guard. For three centuries a soldier in war, a civilian in peace -- of security and honor, I am the custodian, now and forever... I am the Guard.

This document, produced for a National Guard celebration, provided a one-page summary in both words and pictures of the history of the National Guard.

IMAGES
of America

HUDSON'S NATIONAL GUARD MILITIA

William L. Verdone and Lewis Halprin

Published by Arcadia Publishing
Charleston SC, Chicago IL, Portsmouth NH, San Francisco CA

Library of Congress Catalog Card Number: 2005935357

For all general information contact Arcadia Publishing at:
Telephone 843-853-2070
Fax 843-853-0044
E-mail sales@arcadiapublishing.com
For customer service and orders:
Toll-Free 1-888-313-2665

Visit us on the Internet at http://www.arcadiapublishing.com

On the cover: Participating in a Memorial Day parade on May 30, 1955, is the tank company of the 181st Infantry Regiment, 26th Yankee Infantry Division. Comdr. Robert J. Rennie and guidon bearer Richard J. Kaloustian are leading the group. Kaloustian remained in the National Guard and became the division command sergeant major. He retired after over 35 years of service. (Courtesy of Joseph W. Lapine.)

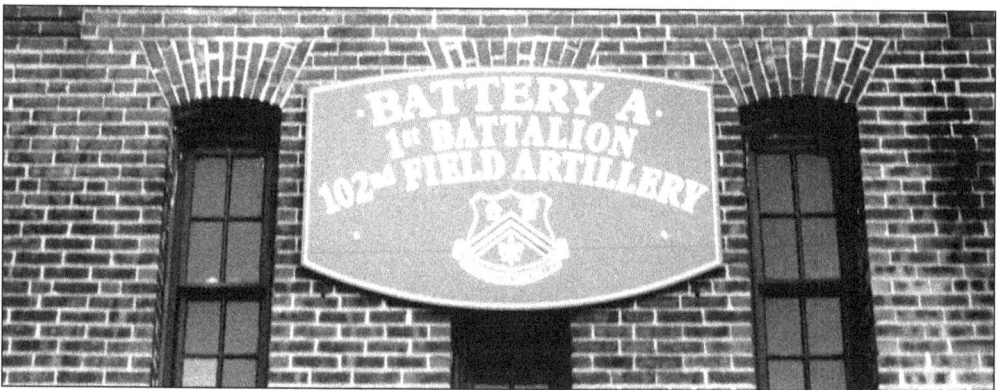

Battery A, 1st Battalion, 102nd Field Artillery, 2nd Corps of Cadets was transferred from Lynn to Hudson in 1995 with 80 men on the roster. They are now headquartered in Quincy. In November 2004, the unit was deployed and trained at Fort Dix in New Jersey before departing for a tour of duty in Iraq during Operation Enduring Freedom. This book is dedicated to Battery A.

CONTENTS

ACKNOWLEDGMENTS

I have been involved with the Hudson National Guard unit and its armory for most of my life. In my senior year of high school, in 1952, I decided to join the unit, which was located near the high school. We drilled one evening each week, and my first assignment was as a wireman and climber. This experience served me well, and I got a similar job with the local Hudson Light and Power Department. I retired as their general line foreman 38 years later.

I am always impressed with the wide range of people who walk into the armory each week—carpenters, teachers, engineers, plumbers, cooks, people of almost every occupation. They use those skills to create a well-oiled military unit capable of working with the latest equipment. The officers help the soldiers become better at their tasks, and the soldiers help the officers become better leaders. There is camaraderie among them that is not always present in regular army units. Although they are prepared to defend the country if necessary, the National Guard is first and foremost a local militia made up of neighbors prepared to provide assistance and protection when a state or local disaster strikes.

Through this book I provide a look at some of these people, their equipment, and their activities through the years. This is not just a troop of soldiers, they are your neighbors. Their first order of business is to protect you, your town, and your state. I am proud to be a member, and I think you will find that this book's selection of pictures and stories reflects my pride. Most of the photographs included here are from my personal collection or from the archives of the Hudson Historical Society, of which I am a member. Additional contributors include the Hudson National Guard, Andrew A. Munter, Camillo DeArchangelis, Gary Smith, Paul V. Boothroyd, and many others.

—William L. Verdone

Every time I go through the center of Hudson my eye is attracted by the armory, a large brick fortress built like a castle on a small hill. I knew it was built in 1910, and because of my fascination with local history I had to find out more. Fortunately, I found Bill Verdone giving a slide show on the armory's history at one of the monthly meetings of the Hudson Historical Society. I discovered that he was involved with the National Guard from his high school days, and he worked his way from a private to a lieutenant colonel during 34 years of service. He spent much of that time with the Hudson National Guard unit as its captain. What I learned through his lectures and personal conversations was fascinating, and I had to find a way to share that information with a larger audience. This book is the result. I am sure you will be as fascinated as I was, even if you were never a member of a military unit. This collection depicts the old units, their uniforms, the equipment, the camps, the parades, the awards, and more. Enjoy!

—Lewis Halprin

INTRODUCTION

This introduction provides historical information about the formation of the National Guard in the state of Massachusetts, and specifically the National Guard unit in Hudson. It also provides a description of what goes on during training sessions at the Hudson National Guard armory, located in the center of Hudson, and what goes on during the unit's 15-day training camp at Fort Drum in New York every summer. The intent of this information is to provide a better understanding of how the pictures shown in the rest of the book fit into the history and activities of this unit.

In 1630, the Massachusetts Bay Colony formed the first military companies. In 1636, the Massachusetts General Court passed laws that brought about the formation of three regimental militia organizations within the colony. Around 1774, they started to use the term Middlesex County Militia. Around 1840, the militia was referred to as the Massachusetts Volunteer Militia, or MVM. Finally in 1907, all organizations of the MVM were designated as the Massachusetts National Guard.

At that time, Hudson was a part of Marlborough known as Feltonville. It had one of the first three regimental militia organizations, and they were called the North Regiment. In 1866, Feltonville separated from Marlborough, was renamed Hudson, and was incorporated as a town. With 41 members signing on, Adelbert A. Mossman organized Company L, 5th Infantry Regiment, 2nd Brigade, Massachusetts Volunteer Militia, also known as the Hudson Light Guard. On November 30, 1921, Company B, 181st Infantry Regiment, 26th Yankee Infantry Division was organized and met at the Hudson armory. According to historical documents, the 181st Infantry Regiment can trace its lineage all the way back to the North Regiment.

The Hudson unit operated from 1907 as part of the National Guard. At the start of World War II in 1941, the unit was federalized (made part of the U.S. Army) and sent off to fight in the war. To provide homeland security, a State Guard was created in Hudson. The State Guard met at the now-vacant armory, were under the control of the governor, and their expenses were paid by the state of Massachusetts. In 1947, a few years after World War II ended, a new National Guard unit was formed, and the State Guard disbanded. This new National Guard unit remained an infantry unit until 1959, when the group became a National Guard armored company. Then, as needs changed in 1988, the unit became a National Guard cavalry troop. Changing once again in 1995, the unit became a National Guard artillery battery.

The Hudson armory was large enough that in 1947 a second unit was formed: a National Guard cannon company. In 1947, that unit was reorganized into a heavy mortar company, and it remained so until it disbanded in 1959.

Since the days since the Hudson Light Guard was formed, the unit went through 20 different reorganizations commanded by 58 captains and three first lieutenants. William L. Verdone, coauthor, was the 43rd of the 61 commanders. Troops from the Hudson unit served during the Spanish American War (1898), the Mexican border campaign (1916), World War I (1917), World War II (1941–1945), and the war in Iraq (2004).

In 1910, the Hudson National Guard armory was built. Early plans for the armory included a recreational area around it that included a place to launch boats on the nearby Assabet River. The armory was lit up every night for drills and non-commissioned officer (NCO) schools. The armory's cavernous drill area was used by the troops but was also frequently used by the town. The town held meetings there, elections, basketball practice and games, high school graduations, junior and senior high school proms, industrial shows, and even Guy Lombardo dinner dances.

After drilling, the troops could play basketball or ping-pong and use the two-lane bowling alley, located in the basement level of the armory. Every armory had a special room set aside for the NCOs that they maintained and decorated for the spirit, morale, welfare, and pride of the unit. It was considered a real privilege for a recruit to be invited into the NCO bar to have a can of beer with friends. Basketball and rifle teams of the regiment competed with each other on nights when they were not drilling. Qualifiers had the distinction of making the regimental rifle or pistol team and competed annually in Wakefield.

The Hudson National Guard armory housed two companies of the 181st Infantry Regiment. The 181st Infantry Regiment is one of the regiments in the 26th Infantry Division of the Massachusetts National Guard. The regiment had a tank company and a heavy mortar company, each with their own company commander.

At one time, the tank company had a tank simulator in a corner of the drill shed floor. The simulator consisted of a tank turret (there was no outside armor), had manual and automatic controls, and it was equipped with a periscope, a telescope, a range finder, and an azimuth indicator. Crews could practice bore sighting and give fire commands, disassembly and assembly the breach (the main gun), and load a dummy round into the breach.

The heavy mortar company practiced with their weapons on the drill shed floor by setting up and tearing down the 4.2-inch mortars with the aid of sandbags. Then, aiming stakes could be placed with the instructions from the aiming circle team and the fire direction center crew.

All personnel had to fire a .22-caliber rifle on the indoor rifle range, located in the basement of the armory. Once a year, ranges were used at Fort Devens, and guards had to qualify on larger weapons, such as the .30-caliber M1 rifle, the .30-caliber carbine, the .45-caliber pistol, the .45-caliber submachine gun, and the 3.5-caliber rocket launcher.

In the 1950s, the units met one night a week. In the 1960s, they started to meet one weekend a month, sometimes just on Saturday, often Saturday and Sunday, and occasionally the whole weekend, starting on Friday night. The majority of this training was centered on the soldier's individual weapons qualification and their military occupation specialty (MOS), whether he was a tank driver, loader, gunner, tank commander, or mortar crewman.

One of the functions the Hudson National Guard was assistance during an emergency within the state. Troops from the Hudson unit served during the big Hudson fire in 1894, the Chelsea fire in 1908, the Lawrence mill strike in 1912, the Salem fire in 1914, the Hurricane of 1938, the Worcester Tornado in 1953, and the Blizzard of 1978.

On Tuesday June 9, 1953, a tornado struck the nearby city of Worcester. The unit was having a normal drill that evening, when they received word from headquarters to pack up and move to a section of Worcester called Greendale, where the funnel had touched down. They could take only a three-day supply of personal items, raincoats, blankets, and ponchos. Arriving in Worcester at about 10:30 p.m., they pitched tents on someone's front lawn and set up security in the area. Looking around in the morning, the troops saw nothing but empty cellar holes on both sides of the street and clothing hanging from the tree branches. The troops were assigned a post to stand guard, and they were provided a challenge and password to identify looters and strangers and keep them out of the area. Anytime a guard observed something suspicious, their sergeant was called. Guards either escorted strangers out of the area or brought the police in to arrest them. The tank company from Hudson went to Westborough, and Company K of Marlboro went to Shrewsbury. Company M of Clinton went to Worcester and Shrewsbury.

Once a year in the summer, a 15-day annual training camp is conducted by all units of the National Guard, in order to achieve the training goals that have been set for that year. Convoys of trucks are formed in order to transport the personal and equipment of each armory down to the training camp area. The Hudson National Guard usually travels to Fort Drum in New York for their camp training.

The preparation and planning prior to going to the camp is part of their annual training. Everything has to be planned for: the food, gasoline, ammunition, water, medical aid stations, and supplies. Maps are marked and refueling points are set up in advance. Drivers are assigned to vehicles, bumpers are marked, and even the speed of the convoys is planned so that departure and arrival times are accurate. Towing and engine repair is provided by the unit's maintenance personnel.

In earlier days, all military convoys had priority on the road. With the help of road guides and police support, and without having to stop for red lights, the Hudson convoy could go through the cities of Albany, Schenectady, and Syracuse on their way to Fort Drum at 40 miles per hour with little disruption. Some years, parts of the 26th Yankee Infantry Division went to camp by train or by bus. In the 1990s, some even went by large C-5 military aircraft, but most units go to camp by truck. In the 1940s, Hudson's tanks were shipped by train on flatbeds, but by the 1960s, special motor pools were set up at Fort Drum that allowed the unit to borrow tanks for use at the training camp rather then transport their tanks from the armory to camp and back.

Once at Fort Drum, the Hudson unit is assigned to a certain area of the army post where their training will be conducted. They are also assigned to ranges where they will fire their weapons.

For the Hudson unit's tank company, a typical training camp starts out on Sunday morning with a daylight tank march. They cross check points on time, travel through deep streams, and plow through muddy places. On Monday, the unit moves to the firing range and conducts live fire exercises. During the camp period, the unit will go on day and night blackout tank marches and tank tactical exercises.

Before the main tank gun can be fired, all the unit's crewmen must pass a tank crewman preliminary gunnery examination to make sure that each crew member knows how to use the guns and equipment in the tank, how to safely handle the ammunition, and how to disassemble and assemble the .30-caliber and .50-caliber machine guns. The men also have to demonstrate that they can work together as a crew when firing the machine guns at a moving target, firing the main tank gun on a moving target, and firing all the tank's weapons at the same time.

During the rest of the week after Hudson's tank crews are qualified, they continue their training by preparing for simulated combat exercises. This starts by checking and repairing, if necessary, each tank's tracks and engine, checking their machine guns, loading ammunition, and setting their radio to the proper frequencies. They are given routes to take to identify and locate targets. The tanks form an attack position and, upon being given the attack order, assault the objection. After a successful attack, the tanks reorganize and get ready for the next attack order.

For those in Hudson's mortar companies, the activity at a typical training camp changed a lot over the years. In the 1950s, the squads did a lot of moving around. They set up their mortars either in an attack posture, a delay posture, or a defend posture. The mortar crews set out their aiming stakes and received instructions from the aiming circle team to set the sights on their mortars. After firing on their target, the mortars were loaded on three-quarter-ton trucks and driven to another location where they were unloaded and set up again immediately. In later years, Hudson's squads skipped this practice and went directly into the field for the entire two weeks, marrying up with infantry personnel from other units and performing combined arms exercises with live fire. Tactics became even more realistic when the unit had to face simulated aggressor troops.

This introduction has provided information on what the National Guard units do in general, and what the Hudson National Guard does in particular during their monthly weekend training in the armory and during their 15-day training camp at Fort Drum. It is hoped that this background information will help you better understand the historic pictures that fill the rest of this book.

The National Guard used many insignias to identify the unit to which its members were assigned. Starting with the upper left insignia and going clockwise is the infantry insignia of Company M, Massachusetts Volunteer Militia; the infantry insignia of Company M, Massachusetts National Guard, from 1907 to 1921; the infantry and the powder horn insignia created during a reorganization in 1921 of Company B, 181st Infantry Regiment; the shoulder and unit insignia of Company F, Massachusetts State Guard, from 1941 to 1946; the infantry and the powder horn insignia in 1947 of the tank company of the 181st Infantry Regiment; the crossed sabers with tank collar and unit insignia for Company B, 1/110 Armor; the crossed sabers collar and shoulder unit insignia for Troop A, 1/110 Cavalry; and the crossed cannons collar and unit insignia for Battery A, 1st Battalion, 102 Field Artillery. In the center is the last shoulder insignia of the 26th Yankee Infantry Division, which disbanded in 1993. (Insignias courtesy of the Hudson Historical Society, William L. Verdone, Andrew A. Munter, George S. Preston, and Battery A.)

One

INFANTRY

Hudson's militia was an infantry unit for 97 years, from 1862 to 1959. The infantry branch, known as "the Queen of Battle," has a mission to find, fix, and destroy the enemy by fire and maneuver. There was a movement at the Massachusetts State House to convert Hudson to a tank unit in 1920, but that failed because the townspeople objected to the idea. The divisions changed in 1959, from the old square structure of four regiments to the new triangular concept of three regiments. This new structure was known as the pentomic division. (Insignias courtesy of the Hudson Historical Society and William L. Verdone.)

Capt. William E. C. Worcester is standing in front of the 40-member Company I, 5th Infantry Regiment, 2nd Brigade, Massachusetts Volunteer Militia, sometime around June 1, 1862. The town of Hudson was then known as Feltonville. The uniforms consisted of dark-blue frock coats and light-blue trousers with forage or fatigue caps. (Courtesy of Mary Eleanor Fillmore.)

Company M, 1st Battalion, 5th Infantry Regiment, 2nd Brigade, Massachusetts Volunteer Militia, also known as the Hudson Light Guard, is pictured on their return from New York City on May 2, 1889. They are standing in front of what is now the Hudson Savings Bank. Adelbert A. Mossman was their captain from 1888 to 1896. (Courtesy of the Hudson Historical Society.)

Company M is assembled on May 6, 1894. Harry C. Moore, seated in the middle of the first row, is shown with the chevron stripes of a sergeant. Shortly after, in June 1894, he was promoted to second lieutenant. During these years, the men met and voted by ballot to elect their captain and officers. Men's titles were musicians, artificers, and wagoners. (Courtesy of the Hudson Historical Society.)

This 1901 picture shows all the officers in the 5th Infantry Regiment. In the back row, fourth from the left, is Lewis E. Ordway, a first lieutenant in 1900. Capt. Harry Moore is in the first row, seventh from the left. (Courtesy of the Hudson Historical Society.)

Members of Company M are at the armory after returning from the Mexican border on October 27, 1916. Note the large recruiting sign on the right. (Courtesy of the Hudson Historical Society.)

Capt. Fred B. Dawes and his wife are standing in front of the armory after he returned from the Mexican border on October 27, 1916. (Courtesy of the Hudson Historical Society.)

Members of Company M are shown at the armory after returning from the Mexican border on October 27, 1916. (Courtesy of the Hudson Historical Society.)

Company M is marching into the armory on their return from the Mexican border on October 27, 1916. Boy Scouts are lined up on both sides of the walkway. Fred B. Dawes was captain when Company M was mobilized on June 19, 1916, and mustered into federal service on June 26, 1916, in Framingham. The unit arrived in El Paso, Texas, on July 2, 1916, to patrol the Mexican border. They were relieved on November 11, 1916, spending only four months on this duty. Note the blanket rolls covered by the shelters, which are half slung over the guards' shoulders. (Courtesy of the Hudson Historical Society.)

Members of Company M are at the rear of the armory with a team of horses and a wagon. Notice the writing on the canvas: "M Co. 5th Reg. Inf. Mass." When they arrived in South Framingham on June 23, 1916, they needed a team of horses to pull the wagon to the camp. A dozen men volunteered before a team of mules was brought to do the job. Note the canvas tents sticking out of the front of the wagon next to the driver. (Courtesy of the Hudson Historical Society.)

Company M is seen waiting at a train station to return home on March 1, 1912. Since February 17, 1912, the unit had been on strike duty at the mills in Lawrence. Capt. Harry C. Moore moved Company M, with 60 men and three officers, to Lawrence on Saturday, February 17. They took

the 9:07 a.m. train from the Fitchburg Division Station on Main Street and met the rest of the 1st Battalion when they arrived at North Station in Boston, before leaving for Lawrence. (Courtesy of the Hudson Historical Society.)

This picture is a continuation of the picture shown on the previous page. The unit was on strike duty at the American Woolen Company, which at that time employed 6,400 hands at three mills: the Oswoco Mills, Ayer Mills, and the Wood Mill. They returned home after 16 days and

received $24.80 pay. It is said that the women pickets were more abusive and worse to deal with than the men's. (Courtesy of the Hudson Historical Society.)

Pictured is an M4A3 Sherman tank with a 76-millimeter gun. This guard is making certain the driver's hatch is locked in position before he enters the driver's compartment. On a drill night, the driver would take the tank from the maintenance shed beside the armory and drive up Park Street to Brigham Street to a sand pit. (Courtesy of Andrew A. Munter.)

Here, the M4A3 Sherman tank's tube is tied down in travel lock over the front of the tank. In later tank models, the gun is tied down over the engine compartment. (Courtesy of Andrew A. Munter.)

The M4A3 Sherman tank is getting ready to move. The tank commander is giving last-minute instructions to the gunner on the left and the driver on the right. The tank commander enters the fighting compartment above and behind the gunner. (Courtesy of Andrew A. Munter.)

The driver is checking the travel lock, which holds down the gun while the tank is moving so as not to damage the recoiling mechanism. Andrew A. Munter is inspecting the locking device of the gunner's hatch. Should these hatches swing closed while a person is standing with his head out of the hatch, he may loose his head or get a pretty good bruise. (Courtesy of Andrew A. Munter.)

The M4A3 Sherman tank has an old bogie wheel suspension system. Notice that a sprocket with teeth is located at the front of the tracks. Four tanks can be seen on the tank range, ready to fire the .30-caliber machine guns. (Courtesy of Andrew A. Munter.)

A tank is rolling up in this photograph. While the gun is in travel lock, the turret cannot move. A .50-caliber machine gun is mounted on the top, outside the tank commander's position. Spare track pads are hanging outside on the turret wall. There are many eyes and hooks for towing on the front of the tank, in case it gets stuck. (Courtesy of Andrew A. Munter.)

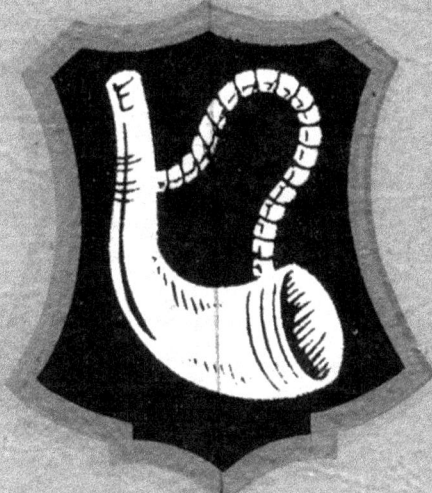

LESSON PLAN

HEAVY MORTAR COMPANY

181 ST. INFANTRY REGIMENT

IF THE MEN HAVE NOT LEARNED .
THE INSTRUCTOR HAS NOT TAUGHT.

This is a protective cover for a lesson plan used by the heavy mortar company of the 181st Infantry Regiment, 26th Yankee Infantry Division, from 1948 to 1958. The unit was known as a cannon company in 1947. The lesson plan would have been presented to the inspecting officer in this manner while the class was in progress.

Company M is assembled in 1917 for their regimental picture. Capt. Mark Smith, with over 30 years of service, was just recently assigned, and he would muster the men for military service. While awaiting their orders, from July 27 to August 17, 1917, the men pitched pyramid tents at the rear of the armory. One hundred forty-nine men and three officers then boarded three passenger coaches at the train station and went to Framingham. All but 18 men amalgamated

with the 9th Infantry, which became known as Company M, 101st Infantry, and were in France by October 12, 1917. They served 18 months overseas and returned home on February 14, 1919. Soon after, other men were assigned to the company, and they left Framingham on November 23, 1917, for Charlotte, North Carolina. (Courtesy of the Hudson Historical Society.)

This 1953 photograph is of the heavy mortar company of the 181st Infantry Regiment, also known as the regimental commander's artillery. The group gained its federalization in 1947 as a cannon company but was reduced 12 years later, in 1959, to a mortar platoon within a headquarters company. The 72-man Hudson unit came from the surrounding towns of Clinton,

Marlboro, Maynard, Stow, and Westborough. Pictured are William Lesieur (first row on the left) and 1st Lt. Robert F. Waugh (first row, seventh from the left), the company commander. This year, machetes were replaced by entrenching tools. A new GMC hydromantic drive two-and-a-half-ton truck was given to the guards. (Courtesy of William Lesieur.)

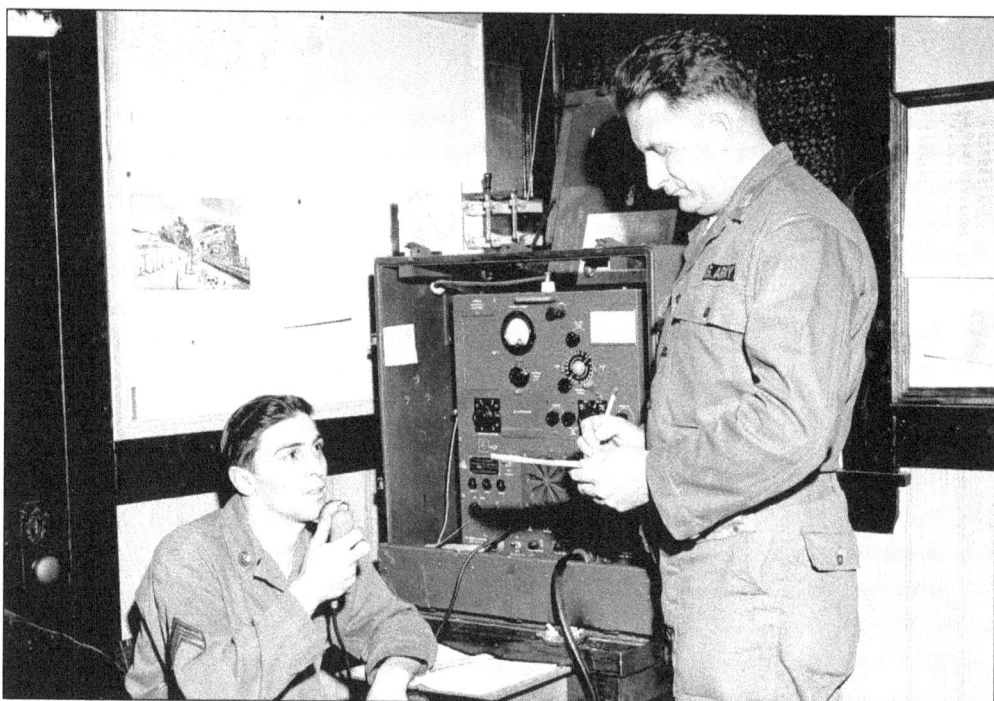

The main radio in the armory was used by the tank company of the 181st Infantry Regiment, 26th Yankee Infantry Division to contact higher-ranking headquarters. It was also used for radio communications classes. Cpl. Richard Corrinni is talking into the microphone, and CWO Anthony M. Kurgan Sr. is writing the incoming message in 1953. (Courtesy of Joseph W. Lapine.)

During a drill in September 1954, the heavy mortar company's mission was to secure the area around the generation plant of the Hudson Light and Power Department on Cherry Street, the town's only power supply. The radio pictured is an AN/PRC-10, which transmitted well from distances of 10 to 15 miles. From left to right are 1st Lt. Robert F. Waugh (the commander), Cpl. William L. Verdone, and 2nd Lt. Herbert E. LaCroix. The 26th Yankee Infantry Division was nearly activated during the Korean War. (Courtesy of Dorothy M. Waugh.)

An M47 turret trainer sat on the drill shed floor of the armory in Hudson in 1955. It could traverse manually or automatically and had instruments and radios just like the fighting compartment of a real tank. The breech could also be disassembled. Shown from left to right are Charles W. Mosher, Charles Gooligan, Ronald A. Stokes, and Richard Deberadinis. The instructor to the far right is unidentified. (Courtesy of Ronald A. Stokes.)

Peter R. Pekkala is giving arm and hand signals as an M48A1 tank moves in the bivouac area in 1958. It must be a non-tactical day because the guards are not wearing steel helmets. The main gun is bolted down to the rear in travel lock position. The fender still has "181 INF" painted on it. Clyde Wheeler and Bruce R. Warila are riding on the turret. (Courtesy of Clyde Wheeler.)

The first two tanks pictured have bulldog faces painted on the right side of the turret, and blue pennants fly from the radio antenna. In 1966, the radio call sign was "bulldog." Here, Lt. Col. James F. Young has ordered 15 tanks to the field. Joining the column are a maintenance personnel carrier, medic personnel carrier, and an M88 recovery vehicle, in addition to the wheeled vehicles. Guards wore nose bandanas to keep the dust out. (Courtesy of M.Sgt. Harry A. Millman.)

These troops are standing in front of typical World War II barracks at Pine Camp in New York, in 1952. A fire guard was always on duty, as the estimated time for this wooden structure to burn down was four minutes. It was standard operating procedure (SOP) to have a fire drill to see how fast the barracks could be emptied. The barracks all had iron stoves fed with coal, so guards could take a hot shower. It was always a problem to find dry wood or coal to burn. Maintenance personnel in the New York consite had photographs on the wall showing snow as high as the overhanging roof above the first floor. To exit, they tunneled from the barracks to the street. Most wooden buildings have been replaced with brick structures because the U.S. Army Mountain Division trains here in the winter. The most northern end of the post reaches Canada.

The newest streamers are displayed that will be attached to the guidon of the tank company of the 181st Infantry, who were returning home from Pine Camp in 1951. In 1954, Armando R. Silva would transfer to Fort Devens and work as a full-time National Guardsmen in the maintenance shop with the 726th Maintenance Battalion. Those in the photograph who would remain for their military pay after serving 20 years or more are Raymond Garcia, Anthony M. Kurgan Sr., Harry A. Millman, John L. Naze, Hubert E. Lacroix, Richard J. Kaloutian, Armando R. Silva, James E. Davis, and Donald R. Metivier. (Courtesy of Armando R. Silva.)

Two

ARMOR

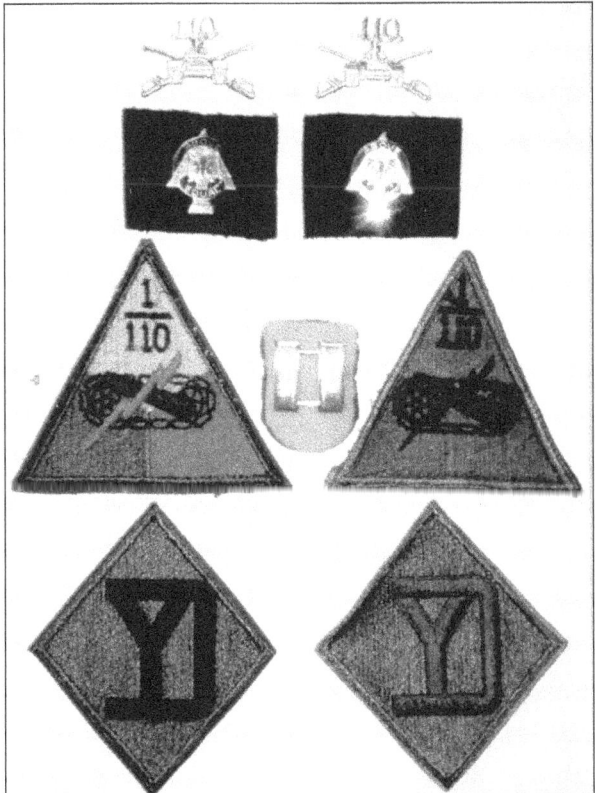

Formed in 1951, the mission of the armor branch is to destroy enemies with firepower, mobility, and shock action. During the pentomic division change in 1959, Hudson became an armored unit within a tank battalion. That year, the heavy mortar company was reduced to a mortar platoon within a headquarters company. The Hudson unit remained as a tank company for 29 years, from 1959 to 1988. (Insignias courtesy of George S. Preston.)

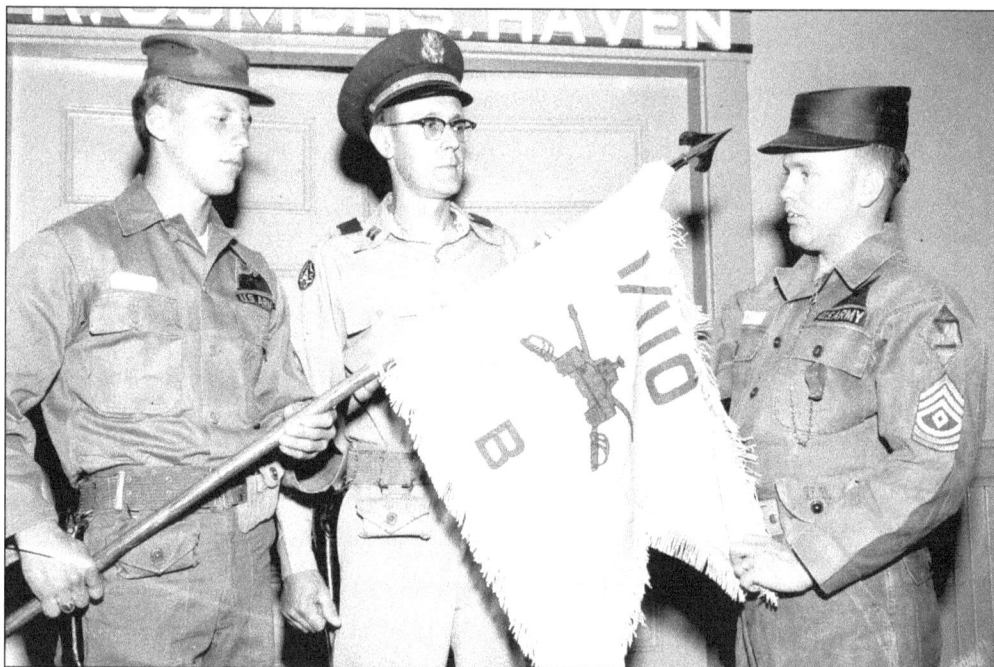

On May 1, 1959, the 26th Yankee Infantry Division changed as a result of the pentomic division. The tank company of the 181st Infantry Regiment became Company B. Shown from left to right are Spc. Bruce Warila (shown holding the new guidon), Capt. Robert J. Rennie, and 1st Sgt. Raphael McDonald. Officers could now wear the insignias of the armor branch. (Courtesy of Joseph W. Lapine.)

On May 1, 1959, there were five tank companies in the state: Company A in Clinton, Company B in Hudson, Company C in Concord, Company D in Saugus, and Company E in Stoneham. The headquarters company in Framingham became known as the 1st Medium Tank Battalion, 110th Armor, 26th Yankee Infantry Division. Shown from left to right are 1st Lt. Earl Leonard and Capt. Rennie. (Courtesy of Joseph W. Lapine.)

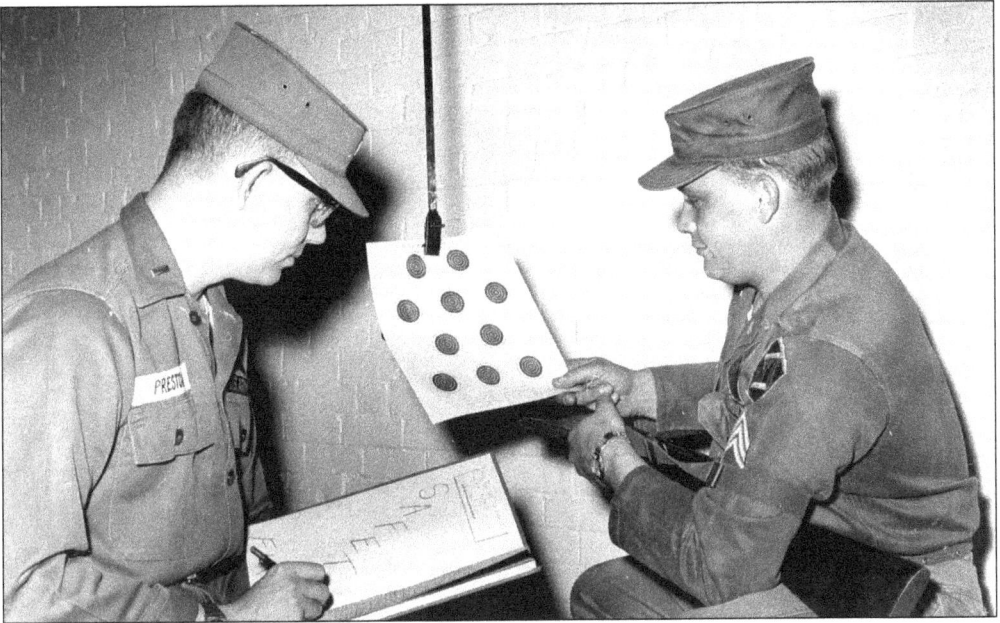

The Hudson armory had a two-point, 80-foot-long indoor firing range in the basement where .22 caliber rifle familiarization and state indoor competitions could be held. Shown in 1959, from left to right, are 1st Lt. George S. Preston and Sgt. Curtis A. Kennedy. (Courtesy of Joseph W. Lapine.)

Company B's equipment is stored in the radio room of the Hudson armory, in 1959. A corner of the room is shown, where the infantry AN/GRC-7 and AN/GRC-8 band radios were stored along with telephones, a switchboard, and wire. Spc. Edward N. Jenson is pictured. (Courtesy of Joseph W. Lapine.)

Members of Company B are maintaining their tank. Tightening the track pads and wedge nuts of the M48 tanks at the end of the day was dirty maintenance, and all crews were required to participate. The tracks would also be greased. In 1959, the tank battalion trained at Camp Drum in New York, and the tanks were drawn from the New York equipment consite. Before, the tanks were loaded at Fort Devens and shipped by rail to New York. The army learned how to do this by watching the Ringling Brothers and Barnum & Bailey circus. Tanks would have to drive over many flat cars before reaching their position, and they were then tied down. There are five sets of double support rollers, which the center guides pass through as the track moves. Looking closely, there are six sets of double road wheels. The wheel off the ground near the front is the compensating idler. At the rear is the drive sprocket. (Courtesy of Joseph W. Lapine.)

Company A, 1st Medium Tank Battalion (Patton), 110th Armor, 26th Yankee Infantry Division, formerly the mortar company of Clinton, is participating in a field exercise at Camp Drum in 1959, the year they changed division. They are learning tank formations by arm and hand signals. Intercoms were still used by crew members and radios were still used to communicate between tanks for safety reasons. This was farmland at one time, and there were many old empty cellar holes that the tanks had to avoid. The terrain is great for tanks, and judging from the mud on the tracks, it is wet. Sitting on the ground are Robert F. Ercolani, Ronald R. Soderlund, Paul V. Coulombe, Bruno Martucci, William E. Thurber, and Henry Estabrook. (Courtesy of the *Boston Globe*.)

On August 1, 1961, this picture was taken at Camp Drum of the 1st Platoon, Company B. They are positioned in front of an M48 tank in the tank park, just before a tactical tank road march. Pictured, from left to right, are the following: (first row) Ronald A. Stokes, Bruce R. Warila, Rene J. Buteau, Royce P. Greenwood, and Robert P. Guay; (second row) Charles Mosher, Jerry Davis, William F. Pomphrey, Henry D. Barber Jr., James Hanson, Curtis Kennedy, Peter Pekala, and Donald V. Rutkowski; (third row) Richard E. Rixford, Francis McNally, and Francis T. Garcia. The fatigue hat is known as a Ridgeway cap. Those fortunate enough got a pair of goggles to wear. The radio headsets were uncomfortable to wear under a steel helmet. The tanker's helmet was not designed yet. (Courtesy of James Hanson.)

Spc. Robert P. Guay is on the ground passing a 90-millimeter round to Rene J. Buteau on the deck of the tank. The primer on top is protected by a hand at all times. Company B was firing at stationary targets, Table IVA, at Camp Drum during annual training in 1961.

Co B 1" Bn 110" Armor, 26 Inf Division
Hudson, MA
1960
Loading live round on M48A1 Tank
Camp Drum NY
L to R
Hayes, Robert Guay
Cover that primer at all times. 90mm round

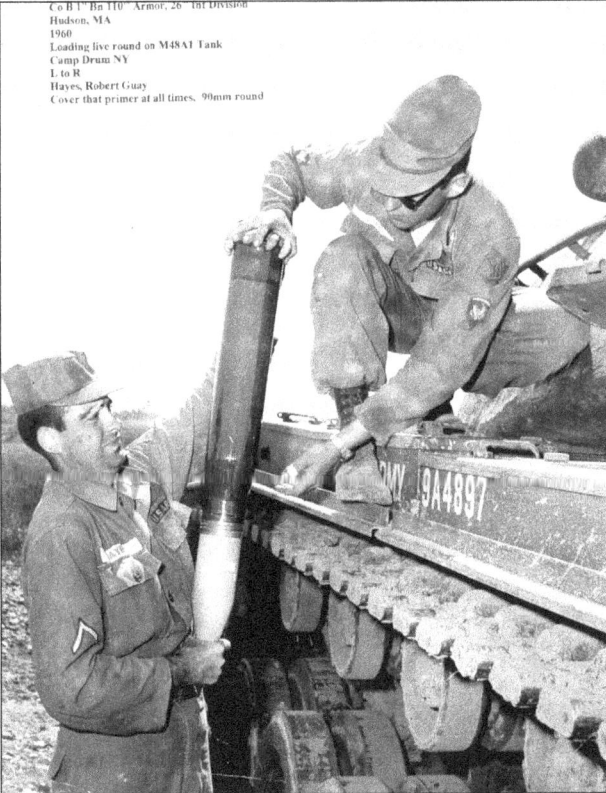

Pvt. Thomas Hayes is handing a 90-millimeter round from the tarp to Spc. Guay on the deck. Guay will then pass the round though the loader's hatch to the loader inside the turret. Company B is training on stationary targets, Table IVA, at Camp Drum in 1960. (Courtesy of Robert P. Guay.)

Spc. Edward J. Hanson is showing the targets in the impact area to Bruce R. Warila behind the .50 caliber machine gun as Royce P. Greenwood remains in radio contact with the officer in charge (OIC) in the tower. Company B was firing Table VIA, crew machine gun exercises, at Camp Drum during annual training in 1960. (Courtesy of Bruce R. Warila.)

A massive recruiting drive was held just before Christmas in 1960. Teams were sent to knock on the doors of potential recruits in neighboring towns. These 11 recruits took the oath and joined Company B. From left to right are Robert Broderick, Donald Prescott, Clyde McAllister, Paul V. Boothroyd, Robert Tobin, John Amirault, Richard DeBeradinis, Joseph Mason, Francis Quinn Jr., Robert Dumas, and Walter Sokolowski. (Courtesy of Joseph W. Lapine.)

This unhappy tank crew in 1961 was eliminated from a first army proficiency test. The safety NCO changed the head spacing of their .50 caliber machine gun, and the weapon did not fire. Shown from left to right are Spc. Joseph Mason (loader), Lt. Col. William A. Thompson (battalion commander), 2nd Lt. William L. Verdone (tank commander), Richard E. Rixford (gunner), and Pvt. Conrad Rainville (driver). The football helmets had built-in earphones. Later, the army would develop a tanker's helmet. (Courtesy of Company B, 1/110 Armor, 26th Infantry Division.)

This Company B tank crew is getting ready to move on line with their tank at Camp Drum in 1963. They are stuffing cotton in their ears for protection. From left to right are Sgt. Jerome Goedecke, Sgt. Richard Rixford, and Sgt. Roger Sabourin. (Courtesy of Jerome Goedecke.)

In 1965, members of Cub Scout Pack No. 3 from Hudson were invited to watch while Company B fired Tables I, II, and III on the .30 caliber machine gun on M Range at Fort Devens. The adults pictured, from left to right, are 1st Lt. Frank W. Putnam III, safety officer; ?; Anne McClellan, den mother; Marguerite Jenkins; 1st Lt. William L. Verdone, OIC of the range; and Paul Mutti, who was Scout master at the time and also a member of the headquarters company of 1/110 Armor in Worcester. On the left is the control tower with a speaker phone and flag set up. Notice every Cub Scout that day was in full uniform. (Courtesy of Anne McClellan O'Connor.)

In 1963, Gov. Endicott Peabody, commander-in-chief of the armed forces in Massachusetts, visited Company B in their motor pool on the day the tanks were returned to the New York consite. The son of the governor was taken for a short ride in one of the M48A1 tanks. When the tank stopped, a loud noise was heard and a torsion bar in the suspension system broke. The crew, with the assistance of maintenance, had to replace the torsion bar before the tank was returned to the New York consite at Camp Drum. On the far right, with a hand on his hip, is battalion commander Lt. Col. William A. Thompson. That year, there were two fathers and sons and three sets of brothers in this company. (Courtesy of Spc. Paul V. Boothroyd.)

The evaluator wearing the white armband observes the unit throughout the day. His rating will be announced later to the commander. The next day will then be an opportunity for the guard to improve on all his ratings. Pictured in 1977, from left to right, are PSG Anthony M. Kurgan Jr., battalion CSM Donald S. Langille, Sfc. Danforth (the evaluator), and Capt. Benjamin L. Benoit III. Langille was a distinguished rifle shot in the division, winning trophies at Camp Curtis Guild and Camp Perry Matches in Ohio. (Courtesy of Anthony M. Kurgan Jr.)

From left to right, Spc. Richard P. Savage, S.Sgt. George P. McNamara, and S.Sgt. Michael J. Callahan from Company B are being tested on an old range finder in 1967. This device tests a guard's ability to range to a target, as determined by the instructor. The range finders got better through the years. (Courtesy of Company B, 1/110 Armor, 26th Infantry Division.)

Pictured in 1965, 1st Lt. William L. Verdone is standing beside a three-ton Ford tank at the Patton Museum at Army Armor School in Fort Knox, Kentucky. After a parade in 1919, a demonstration was staged on South Street and a tank climbed over the barricades. The newspaper then called it a six-ton tank. All of the tanks during World War I were made and used by the French.

The National Guard Centennial Military Ball was held at the Hudson armory on May 21, 1966. From left to right are 1st Lt. William L. Verdone, commanding officer of Company B; Capt. Raymond J. Garcia of Company C in Concord; Col. James Young, battalion commander of the 1st Medium Tank Battalion (Patton) in Worcester; and Capt. George S. Preston of Company A in Clinton. (Courtesy of Hudson Historical Society.)

After a busy week, the commanders are comparing notes and discussing the second week of bivouac in the mess hall at base camp. Pictured from left to right are Company B commander Capt. William L. Verdone, Company B executive officer 1st Lt. Robert J. Reed, Company C commander Frank W. Putnam III, and Company A commander Capt. Ronald F. White. (Courtesy of Company B, 1/110 Armor, 26th Infantry Division.)

This 1977 picture shows Capt. Benjamin L. Benoit III (with the black beret), commander of Company B at Fort Drum in 1977. His rank is displayed on his beret flash, and, at this time, subdued insignias were worn on uniforms instead of brass. Beginning in 1974, only the tank company was authorized to wear the black beret. Today, members of all branches of the U.S. Army must wear the black beret. Captain Benoit is using one of the new single-side AN/VRC-12 transistor radios. To use the radio, authentication tables were required to enter the net. The jeep pictured is an M151, with an independent suspension system. The cupola on the turret is different than the M48 tanks. (Courtesy of Company B, 1/110 Armor, 26th Infantry Division.)

From left to right, Jack Kenny (in the cooks hat), 2nd Lt. Paul R. Czapienski, Joseph Jacobs, and John Amirault from Company B are washing pots and pans after a company party in 1984. When the armory was built, the kitchen was designed to feed 300 men or more. After waiting in the mess line, personnel ate in the mess hall in the next room. Usually, once a year all the officers would assist in the cleanup of the kitchen. That tradition still goes on today. (Courtesy 1st Sgt. Roy Bull, Company B, 1/110 Armor.)

The kitchen personnel have just served meals from the two-and-a-half-ton truck in the center of the image. This is an assembly area where the mechanized infantry have just arrived in their M113 personnel carriers (PCs) before conducting a field exercise at Fort Drum in 1984. The M48 tanks can be identified by the T-shaped blast deflector on the front of the tube. (Courtesy S.Sgt. Gregory A. Boulanger.)

The mess section has just arrived with food in the trailer. This group just returned from the showers at Fort Drum in 1984. Notice the one-quarter-ton Willys jeep and two-and-a-half-ton diesel hydromantic truck. (Courtesy of S.Sgt. Gregory A. Boulanger.)

PSG Anthony M. Kurgan Jr., standing on the turret of an M48A5 tank in 1977, is putting the radio antennas together. Because there are two radio transmitters, two sets of antennas are needed. It only takes a few branches to break the silhouette of the tanks. Two machine guns are mounted on the turret fed by belts of blank ammunition, which make the exercise more realistic. S.Sgt. John I. Kenny Jr. is test firing one of the machine guns. This diesel powered tank has a 105-millimeter gun. It also has a M73 7.62-caliber coaxial machine gun that can be fired by the gunner from within the turret and an M85 .50-caliber machine gun that can be fired from the outside. The five-gallon water can strapped to the turret is for hygienic washing. A plastic container of mosquito protection is on Kenny's helmet. (Courtesy of Anthony M. Kurgan Jr.)

PSG Anthony Kurgan Jr., talking on the radio with the OIC of the range, is displaying a green and orange flag from the turret, indicating the tank has a malfunction and all weapons are clear. The driver is getting ready to move the tank off the firing line. The shiny ball near the top of the turret, known as the ears, act as the ears of the range finder. While firing the main gun, personnel are cautioned not to move in front of the ears because of the risk of getting a concussion. Only four of the five sets of smaller support rollers on the tank can be seen. Center guide teeth move between the support rollers and double road wheels and keep the track centered. Two vertical shock absorbers can be seen near the front. Torsion bar arms can be seen between the road wheels. Kurgan would later transfer and become the command sergeant major of the division. (Courtesy of Anthony M. Kurgan Jr.)

This M577 command post carrier is being shown on the front lawn of the armory at an open house in 1977. Standing on the rear gate, which has been lowered to the ground, from left to right are 2nd Lt. Stephen G. Ross, 2nd Lt. John M. Gralton, Capt. Benjamin L. Benoit III, potential recruit Walter Zina, and Alfred Staal. (Courtesy of Benjamin L. Benoit III.)

Sfc. Ronald W. Gazzaniga, standing on the left, is giving instructions to his crew about equipment stored on the outside racks. Before any tank firing begins, this area must be clear in case of a misfire. The range is closed while the misfire is removed from the turret and the safety officer carries it to a misfire pit at the end of the firing line. (Courtesy of William J. Rivers.)

This M48 tank is being gassed up by a two-and-a-half-ton tanker truck in 1984. Except for detail who are refueling the tank, everyone remains a safe distance away. Smoking is not allowed during this process. The more difficult method was to pump 200 gallons by hand. The tanker truck provides a grounding wire that is attached to the tank. Fire extinguishers are always present during the gassing. (Courtesy of S.Sgt. Gregory A. Boulanger.)

Dismounted infantry troops of the 181st Infantry Regiment are participating in a combined arms fire exercise at Fort Drum in 1965. Rifles and machine guns fired blank ammunition. The tank crews moved ahead and fired 90-millimeter blank rounds, as seen by the smoke. The control officer can be seen with his radio in the jeep on the lower right.

This tank crew of Company B is cleaning the 105-millimeter main gun in 1977. It usually takes three or four men to push the rammer through the tube. The main gun now has a bore evacuator in the middle instead of a T-shaped blast deflector. A crewman is wearing the new tankers helmet. (Courtesy of 1st Sgt. Roy Bull, Company B, 1/110 Armor.)

William Rivers (left) and David Gillespie from Company B are taking a lunch break at Fort Drum in 1977. They are eating off the hood of an M151 jeep.

Three

CAVALRY, ARTILLERY, AND STATE GUARD

The cavalry branch, known as the eyes and ears of the army, has a mission to conduct reconnaissance of the enemy, to gain intelligence on their location, strength, and disposition. The military downsized in the late 1980s and closed down bases across the country. Massachusetts followed by closing down armories and eliminating units. The Clinton armory was shut down, but Hudson was spared by converting to a cavalry unit in 1988. Hudson remained a cavalry troop for seven years, from 1988 to 1995. (Insignia and beret flash courtesy of S.Sgt. Bruce Verdone.)

The cavalry squadron is shown presenting their colors on August 1, 1996, on the parade field opposite the Concord armory. This was the final end of the squadron. In 1993, the 26th Yankee Infantry Division, famous since World War I, was inactivated when the U.S. Army completely reorganized. (Courtesy of S.Sgt. Richard A. Erenius.)

The reviewing stand and dignitaries are watching the cavalry squadron case their colors on the parade field on August 1, 1996. (Courtesy of S.Sgt. Richard A. Erenius.)

One final salute is rendered by the cavalry squadron commander on August 1, 1996, on the parade field. The guidon is down at the position of present arms. Casing the colors follows. (Courtesy of S.Sgt. Richard A. Erenius.)

Color bearers are passing on the colors to the Joint Force Headquarters of the Massachusetts National Guard on August 1, 1996, on the parade field. The Guard began adapting to light brigades. Some divisions had units in three states. (Courtesy of S.Sgt. Richard A. Erenius.)

Troop A of the 110th Cavalry Squadron, at a range at Fort Drum in 1993, are dismounting the M113 armored personnel carriers (APCs). The ramps are already dropped on the first and last carriers. The M113s are equipped with tube-launched, optically-sighted, and wire-guided missiles (TOW). Ammunition is put in one pile and has not been distributed to each vehicle. (Courtesy of Lt. Col. Gary Smith.)

The M113 APC on the left has its ramp lowered to the ground, and the platoon leader is studying the map to identify targets. The other carriers have only the door open and locked back in place. This is to prevent lowering the ramp by mistake, which might break the hinges. The man on top of the fourth APC is positioning the TOW missile. (Courtesy of Lt. Col. Gary Smith.)

This man is walking on the M88 recovery vehicle dozer blade after reeling in the winch line. A 50-ton boom lies on the top of the M88, spare track pads are near the left front side, and a spare road wheel and tow cables are attached. There is a stiff leg boom near the left rear. A .50-caliber machine gun is mounted on top. (Courtesy of Lt. Col. Gary Smith.)

This M60A3 tank is ready to progress along a tank proficiency course. Both a red and a green flag are displayed from the turret. Judging from the tracks in the dirt, plenty of tanks have preceded this one. This tank is equipped with infrared night vision, instead of the old xenon searchlight like the M48A3 tank. (Courtesy of Lt. Col. Gary Smith.)

This light observation helicopter, a Kiowa, is used by the commander to conduct his own aerial reconnaissance. It can also be used by cavalry crewmen to gain information about the enemy location. The artillery fire support coordinator (FSC) assigned to the cavalry can adjust ground firing from this aerial platform. Each helicopter has its own unique sound. As the requirements grew and required more lifting abilities, heavier rotor blades were added. This is not a gun ship like later cobras. Back in the 1950s, Hudson was fortunate to have Lt. Col. William Brown as the division aviation maintenance officer. Col. Richard H. Nanartowich would become the state aviation officer of Otis Air Field at Camp Edwards in the 1970s. One of his assignments was to fly the governor of Massachusetts to Fort Drum. Both officers flew fixed-wing aircraft and helicopters. (Courtesy of Lt. Col. Gary Smith.)

The Cobra helicopter is found in Troop C and D of the 1/110th Cavalry. There are three different payload options: two 7.62-caliber machine guns on each pod, three guided missiles on each pod, or 20 2.5 inch rockets on each pod. A platoon of these cobras is equivalent to a battalion of 105-millimeter howitzers. (Courtesy of Lt. Col. Gary Smith.)

The 1st Air Cavalry Squadron is using its UH-1 helicopters and showing its firing capabilities, including a machine gun, rockets, and guided missiles, at a fire power demonstration by the Army Armor School at Fort Knox in Kentucky in 1965. After the demonstration, the unit was deployed to Vietnam.

Failure to read a terrain map can lead to this situation in a swamp. Eventually, all the blue lines on the map lead from the wetlands to small streams. The tow cables are attached to the tow hooks on the front of the carrier. When the M88 recovery vehicle arrives, the crew will take turns shoveling mud from the bellied M113 carrier. The M88 will drop the front blade and use it as a dead man to pull the vehicle from the mud. (Courtesy of Lt. Col. Gary Smith.)

The last and fourth change for Hudson was for it to become an artillery unit. The artillery branch, known as "the King of Battle," has a mission to provide close, supporting gunfire to the infantry. An artillery unit from Lynn transferred to Hudson in 1995. Hudson has remained an artillery battery since then. (Courtesy of 2nd Lt. John R. Noble.)

Fire direction center personnel are plotting corrections for the new fire mission. No matter how hot it got, T-shirts were never allowed to be worn alone because of the danger of sunburn. Tan T-shirts are better than white ones because they are more camouflaged. (Courtesy of Battery A.)

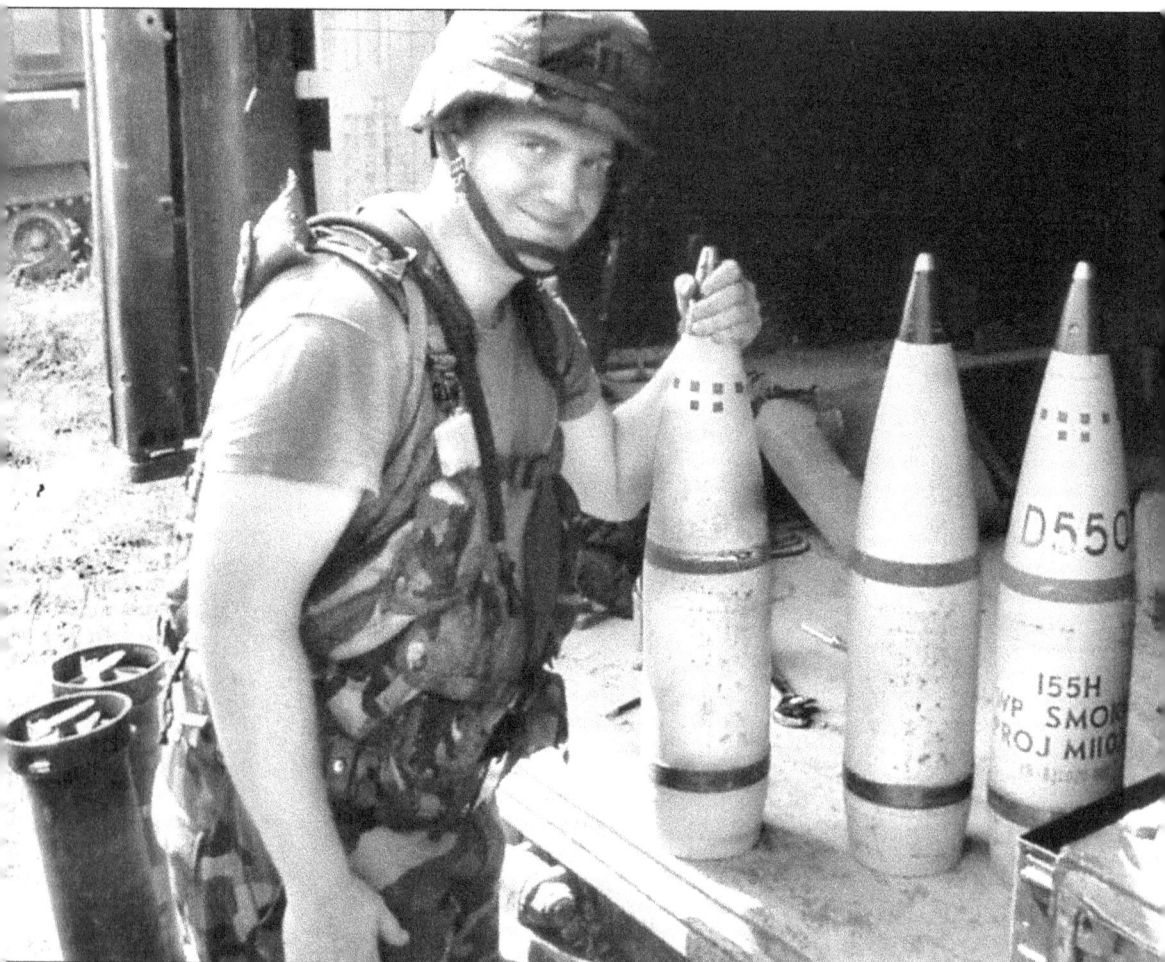

Battery A went to annual training at Fort Drum in 2000, Fort McCoy in Wisconsin in 2001, and Fort Pickett in Virginia in 2002. The fuse can be set on the front of this 155-millimeter howitzer round to explode on contact or be set for time on target (TOT). A hand always covers the primer when it is loaded aboard the howitzer. Then it is strapped down in the ammunition ready rack. It remains covered until it is loaded into the open breach. There must be a mission for "Willy Peter," known as white phosphorus or smoke, after noticing the writing on the shell. All regulations must be met and communications must be established with the guards or the range control officer will not give permission to open the range and fire. (Courtesy of 2nd Lt. John R. Noble.)

Battery A is training with the M109 155-millimeter self-propelled Howitzer, an aluminum-armored, fully-tracked, self-propelled artillery weapon featuring a new extended range howitzer and a 360-degree traversable turret. It provides range and mobility for support of a mechanized or armored division and weighs 21.5 tons. It has a Detroit diesel, eight-cylinder, V-type, 360 horsepower engine, fires one round per minute, has a range of 18,000 meters, a speed of 38 miles per hour, and is also armed with a .50 caliber machine gun. Compared with a tank, this has seven road wheels, no support rollers, a drive sprocket in the front, and a compensating idler wheel in the rear. The engine is in the front, whereas a tank's engine is in the rear. (Courtesy of 2nd Lt. John R. Noble.)

When you are tired, you are tired even when you are in the weapons carrier behind the 155-millimeter self-propelled Howitzer. After the first round has been fired, soldiers may not hear anything for three days. This soldier had KP duty yesterday and sentry duty last night. (Courtesy 1st Sgt. Kenneth L. Rabano.)

This soldier's eyes got too heavy while studying for his next exam at the armory. Exams, given on a computer, must be passed for a guard to achieve a higher rank. (Courtesy of Battery A.)

Men from the combat support company are standing beside the new maintenance building at Camp Edwards. M.Sgt. James Calamare served with Troop A, 1/110th Armor and Battery A, 1/102nd Field Artillery. (Courtesy of M.Sgt. James Calamare.)

The firing day is over and the tube is elevated. The men on the top of the turret are off-loading their duffle bags and closing down the hatches. A canvas tarp on the weapons carrier keeps the ammunition cool and dry. (Courtesy of 1st Sgt. Kenneth L. Rabano.)

Shown above is the rear of the weapons carrier. The fuses are being set on the 155-millimeter rounds as announced by the fire direction center. (Courtesy of Battery A.)

A platoon leader is studying a map before moving his unit to a new location during a tactical exercise. The unit could move as many as six times in one day to new firing positions, depending on whether attacking or delaying actions are taking place. (Courtesy of Battery A.)

An M577 command post vehicle is parked against the tree line with its ramp lowered so that personnel can enter and leave the vehicle. Inside are benches, tabletops, and accommodations for radios. Judging from the number of antennas, it is monitoring six radio nets. The rack on the top front is for a five-kilowatt generator that is used when the engine is not running. The generator usually is set up some distance from the vehicle because of the noise it makes. The trim vane is forward only to store the duffle bags. This trim vane prevents it from going underwater when crossing a river. (Courtesy of Battery A.)

Battery A is getting ready for a tactical road march at Fort Pickett in Virginia. Because of an environmental program on this post, track vehicles must not run over deer seedlings planted along the tank trails. The vehicle commander is manning the .50-caliber machine gun, and the antennas are tied down so they will not be broken by low branches and communications wire. (Courtesy of Battery A.)

This Hudson unit will convert into a 155-millimeter towed howitzer battery in the near future. Its weapon would then be towed by a five-ton truck. The 155-millimeter towed howitzer is being set up on the front lawn of the armory. At this time, they are showing what the maximum elevation would look like. This weapon can fire a distance of up to 15 miles. The long stabilizers behind the gun are open, as seen in front of the truck. (Courtesy of Battery A.)

The 155-millimeter gun, now lowered, is ready to be attached to the truck and towed away. The National Guard is trying to modify and streamline units like this into smaller, faster light brigades, which means they could be air dropped or could parachute from a C-5 aircraft. (Courtesy of Battery A.)

Some house cleaning must be done in between fire missions by the crew of Battery A. The door on the turret is open and trash is being gathered in the plastic bags hanging on the rear of the weapons carrier. (Courtesy of Battery A.)

The stabilizers of the 155-millimeter towed howitzer are closed and attached to the towing eye at the rear of the truck. In a defensive position, the tube can be depressed and fired as a straight trajectory weapon. The unit possesses counter battery equipment, which can plot the return trajectory of the last enemy weapon fired. (Courtesy of Battery A.)

The Massachusetts State Guard is formed during wartime. When the regular National Guard troops are federalized and leave their states, the governor can form a State Guard to take the place of those troops. This happened to Hudson during the years between 1941 and 1946. When World War II was over, the State Guard was dissolved and the regular National Guard unit applied to get its federal recognition back. It then formed as a new unit in Hudson. (Insignias courtesy of Andrew A. Munter.)

This picture, taken in 1941 at a parade in Framingham, shows Massachusetts State Guard member Pvt. Camillo DeArcangelis. The unit was strengthened and grew from 40 to 58 men. They began training students as the Hudson Guard Cadets. (Courtesy of Camillo DeArcangelis.)

After the September 11, 2001, terrorist bombing at the World Trade Center, Jersey barriers were placed around the Hudson armory for security reasons and to block entrances. The picture below shows a 155-millimeter self-propelled Howitzer in front of the maintenance shed beside the armory.

Four

CAMPS

This was the cook for Company M, 5th Infantry Regiment, Massachusetts National Guard, at Camp Whitney in South Framingham from June 21, 1916, to July 2, 1916. The mess tent is set up and almost prepared to serve food. (Courtesy of the Hudson Historical Society.)

Company M became the United States Volunteers in 1898. The unit went to Camp Dalton in South Framingham, where the Massachusetts State Police is located, and then to Greenville, South Carolina. Capt. James P. Clare is standing on the far right wearing shoulder boards. Canvas pouches hang across the shoulders of the guards while they eat their meals. The pointed campaign hat is typical for this period. (Courtesy of the Hudson Historical Society.)

Members of Company M are waiting by the freight station on Main Street at the corner of Broad and Main Streets, across the street from the old Poplins Furniture Store, on June 21, 1916. The steel fence is around Hudson Catholic High School property. On July 2, 1916, they departed on trains for El Paso, Texas, to serve on the Mexican border. (Courtesy of the Hudson Historical Society.)

Members of Company M are switching cars to the New York, New Haven, and Hartford Railroad at the South Sudbury Train Station June 21, 1916. Their destination was Camp Whitney in South Framingham. (Courtesy of the Hudson Historical Society.)

Members of Company M are switching cars to go to Camp Whitney in South Framingham, then on to El Paso, Texas, to serve on the Mexican border. Their uniforms consist of a dark shirt and trousers with leggings. New York, New Haven, and Hartford Railroad can be read on the side of the train. (Courtesy of the Hudson Historical Society.)

Members of Company M pitched tents at Camp Whitney and stayed from June 21, 1916, to July 2, 1916. (Courtesy of the Hudson Historical Society.)

Members of Company M are moving through the food line. Everyone has their cups ready. The food must be hot. There is a stovepipe up ahead by the mess tent. (Courtesy of the Hudson Historical Society.)

Members of Company M and medical staff are standing in front of the field hospital. The nurses are at the far right of the image. Only one doctor is in the group, while the rest of the men are orderlies. (Courtesy of the Hudson Historical Society.)

Members of Company M assemble at Camp Whitney. Uniforms consist of dark shirts and trousers with leggings. The men are learning how to stack rifles in front of the formation. Notice the canteen and gas mask hanging from a cartridge belt. The new arrivals have their bed rolls on the ground, so it is time to pitch tents. (Courtesy of the Hudson Historical Society.)

Members of Company M line up at Camp Whitney where they trained from June 21, 1916 to July 2, 1916.

The cook of Company M at Camp Whitney is preparing for meal time. The company cook is not getting much help setting up the line in the mess tent. There are a lot of pots and pans around. (Courtesy of the Hudson Historical Society.)

Members of Company M, in khaki uniforms, have pitched a big squad tent at Camp Whitney. Notice the vehicle parked under the trees. From left to right are 2nd Lt. Ralph P. Hopkins, Capt. Fred B. Dawes, and 1st Lt. Arthur H. Robbins. (Courtesy of the Hudson Historical Society.)

Members of Company M are making something out of rocks near their tent at Camp Whitney. Notice the barn on the right of this image. (Courtesy of the Hudson Historical Society.)

Members of Company M at Camp Whitney are taking time out of their training to play games. Notice the woman visitor on the left rear center and the boy on the right. (Courtesy of the Hudson Historical Society.)

Members of Company M at Camp Whitney are getting ready for inspection. Horseshoe rolls containing their shelter halves and blankets lie on the ground. (Courtesy of the Hudson Historical Society.)

Members of Company M are standing in front of big squad tents at Camp Whitney in 1916. Roll call is taking place. (Courtesy of the Hudson Historical Society.)

Members of Company M at Camp Whitney in 1916 are talking during a break in training. (Courtesy of the Hudson Historical Society.)

Members of Company M are pitching tents at Camp Whitney in 1916. The men in the first row have M106 bolt action rifles with leather slings. (Courtesy of the Hudson Historical Society.)

A member of Company M is standing at attention among the rest of his unit after pitching their tents at Camp Whitney in 1916. The gadget hanging from the loops of his pants is known as a church key and is used for opening bottles. (Courtesy of the Hudson Historical Society.)

On July 1, 1966, at Camp Drum, Company B tanks have just moved to their firing positions onto the range to fire Table IVA, firing at a stationary target with the main gun. It seems that more tanks are arriving because the far right position has ammunition crates behind it. The tubes are elevated and no range flags are displayed on the turret. The crew of the tank second from the right is just getting into the hatch in the turret. Only one man is behind the line of tanks manning the external phone. A safety officer is in position walking behind the line of tanks. Some ammunition crates have been opened and the rounds are still in their cardboard containers waiting to be distributed to the tarps beside each tank when the proper green flag starts flying. Some firing has been done because the ammunition boxes are uneven.

An M47 tank is rolling down the road in 1949. This tank has an armament consisting of one 90-millimeter gun, two .30-caliber machine guns, and one .50-caliber machine gun. It weighs 48 tons and has a continental 12-cylinder, V-type, 810 horsepower, air cooled engine, a five-man crew, and a top speed of 37 miles per hour. In the 1950s, the armory had an indoor turret trainer on the drill shed floor. Tanks were stored in a large maintenance shed beside the armory. (Courtesy of the tank company of the 181st Infantry Regiment.)

This 1955 picture shows a tank from the tank company of the 181st Infantry. The tank is a M4A3 medium tank with a crew of five, a 75-millimeter gun, two .30-caliber machine guns, and a .50-caliber machine gun. Its maximum speed was 26 miles per hour, and its length was 20 feet seven inches long, nine feet seven inches wide, and nine feet two inches tall. It weighed 30 tons and had a Ford, eight-cylinder, V-type, 450 horsepower engine. Its cruising range was 100 miles. It had bogie wheels and front sprockets. Land owners on Manning and Brigham Streets gave permission for these tanks to conduct driver training on their land before housing developments were built. When World War II began, there were only 66 tanks like this in the U.S. Army. When the war ended, there were 88,410 Sherman tanks in the army. (Courtesy of Andrew A. Munter.)

Some members of the 1955 tank company of the 181st Infantry Regiment are pictured. Andrew A. Munter, on the left, is in the gunner's position on the M4A3 Sherman tank. The main gun is in travel lock over the front of the tank. These tanks had levers for steering. When the intercom radio was not working, they tied ropes around the driver's shoulders. The man on top is Ken Clark, on the right is Richard E. Brickey, and the man in front is Robert Chapman. (Courtesy of Andrew A. Munter.)

Members of Company B's maintenance section are standing beside their M88 recovery vehicle at Camp Drum 1984. On the left is Gregory A. Boulanger. This vehicle has a crew of four men, one .50-caliber machine gun, a top speed of 30 miles per hour, a weight of 56 tons, a 12-cylinder, V-type, 980 horsepower, air cooled engine. It also has a front blade and a 50-ton capacity boom. (Courtesy of S.Sgt. Gregory A. Boulanger.)

An armored vehicle launched bridge (AVLB) was attached to Company B at Camp Drum in 1984. The bridge is carried on top of the tank chassis. The bridge is just starting to unfold and will cover a 60-foot stream or river. It can be driven over and picked up on the other side. It has a two-man crew, a maximum speed of 32 miles per hour, a weight of 64 tons, and a 12-cylinder, V-type, 750 horsepower engine. (Courtesy of S.Sgt. Gregory A. Boulanger.)

Members of Company B are stretching the 60-foot launch bridge to almost its full capacity at Camp Drum in 1984. Tank crews had to learn how to launch the bridge. A steel bailey bridge or pontoon bridge would be built if the river was any wider. (Courtesy of S.Sgt. Gregory A. Boulanger.)

An engineer detail was attached to Company B for a day at Camp Drum to show their combat engineer vehicle with its 280-millimeter cannon that fires a high explosive plastic round at bunkers or uses the blade to dig into fortified positions. The cannon is very short and has no travel lock over the rear deck, like a tank would. The metal boom can be used for many demolition purposes. The sponson boxes on the deck contain many useful tools besides crow bars and shovels. The cannon is in the front, where the heaviest armor is. The engine is in the rear under steel grills for cooling. The two headlights sticking up on the front deck have cat eyes for night blackout driving. (Courtesy of 1st Sgt. Roy Bull.)

The difference between an M60 and an M48 tank is the number of support rollers, which were four and three respectively. They both had six road wheels. The turret has a lower silhouette to shield shaped charges directed at it. The cupola, where the tank commander is seen, is new and has more vision blocks to view the exterior. Instead of a solid olive drab paint job, the tanks are camouflaged. In 2000, they were repainted for desert warfare. (Courtesy of Richard A. Erenius.)

These tanks are driving up to the M range at Fort Devens in 1962, where stationery or moving targets would be engaged. The range had a pulley device so the target could move on a track. Later, frangible ammunition was used because the government built a military housing unit just over the crest of the hill. When children appeared on the crest of the hill, a cease fire would be announced and security guards would be sent out to stop anyone from entering the impact area. (Courtesy of Richard E. Rixford.)

This unit photograph of the anti-tank company of the 181st Infantry Regiment, 26th Yankee Infantry Division was taken on Cape Cod at Camp Edwards during annual training from July 13 through 27 in 1947. The company commander was Capt. Emil L. Dion. The uniforms consisted of summer tans, overseas garrison caps, neckties, and low cuts. Seventeen of the 35 men present for the photograph can be positively identified, from left to right, as follows: (first row) Kurgan, Krysa, Still, Fearing, Dion, and Lacouture; (second row) Kochanski, DiLouro, and Amelotte; (third row) Naze, and Braga; (fourth row) McGorty, and Silva; (fifth row) Sherman, Garcia, Metivier, and Kittredge. In that era, they were known as the brown shoe army. Powder horn insignias were worn on the left side of their garrison caps. That group still talks about the seafood dinners and all the beaches they enjoyed on the long weekend. At this time, there were only 12 regular army divisions and six National Guard divisions. (Courtesy of the anti-tank company of the 181st Infantry Regiment.)

Camp Drum is pictured in 1966 as it looked from the control tower, where the officer in charge is located. Usually only medics and communication personnel are allowed here, besides visiting or inspecting officers. Across the street, tank crews in the assembly area are making last-minute preparations before coming to the firing line. All machine guns have T-blocks in the open receivers.

At Camp Drum in 1966, machine gun ammunition, such as .30 and .50 caliber rounds, in the belts are being checked before it is distributed to the tanks on the firing line. Some crates still remain in the one-quarter-ton trailer.

Members of Company M are at the armory after returning from the Mexican border on October 27, 1916. The man on the right is the company cook, Sgt. George A. Peters. Parked in front of the armory is a 1913 Ford, with a red cross in front of the radiator. The men are wearing World War I campaign hats with broad rims. (Courtesy of the Hudson Historical Society.)

Capt. Harry C. Moore is standing in front of Company M in 1910. This was the first company to occupy the armory after it was built in Hudson in 1910. The armory was built for $50,000. It had a mess area that accommodated 300 people, a bowling alley, shower baths, and an 80-foot rifle range. The armory was built in just one year, while William Brigham, the adjutant general from Hudson, was in office. Sgt. George A. Peters, the mess sergeant, stands in the last row on the right. The front doors with the diamond windows were replaced in 2001. (Courtesy of the Hudson Historical Society.)

This state armory is located in Hudson and is the home of Company M. This picture was taken sometime around 1917. In 1888, an old skating rink was used as an armory. In 1899, the militia used the top floor of town hall for drills. Then, the armory was moved to the opera house on South Street. During the week, the American flag was flown from the pole shown in the tower pictured. Today, the flag is raised on a pole in front of the armory. In 1948, a large maintenance shed was built to the right of the armory and used to store vehicles and tanks. (Courtesy of the Hudson Historical Society.)

Five

DISASTERS

Throughout the years, the Massachusetts National Guard was called out on a number of occasions when major disasters struck the area. The Guard mostly provided protection of property against looters until the area could be secured by local officials. The Guard responded during the Hudson Fire of 1894, the Chelsea Fire of 1908, the Lawrence mill strike of 1912, the Salem Fire of 1914, the Hurricane of 1938, the Worcester Tornado of 1953, and the Blizzard of 1978. Andrew A. Munter of Berlin, a member of Company M, is standing in front of a partially destroyed house on a pile of debris caused by the tornado in Worcester. (Courtesy of Andrew A. Munter.)

The tornado touched down on Tuesday at 4:30 p.m., first striking the community of Petersham, then Barre, Rutland, Holden, Worcester, Shrewsbury, Northboro, Westborough, Fayville, Southboro, Grafton, and Northbridge on June 9, 1953. There were 94 people killed, 1,300 injured, 5,000 damaged buildings, and 650 homes and businesses were reduced to rubble. Property loss was set at $53 million. The Hudson units, the tank company and heavy mortar company of Company K from Marlboro, and Company M of Clinton were called out for 10 days of state duty starting on June 9, 1953. On Uncatena Avenue, shown above, there was nothing left but empty cellar holes on both sides of the street. Clothing and dead bodies were hanging from the tree branches, and some two-by-fours had actually penetrated the trunk of a tree. Other streets struck in this area were St. Nicholas, Osceola, Sachem, Acushnet, Rowena, and Calumet Avenues, Clark and Purchase Streets, and Brandon Road. (Courtesy of Andrew A. Munter.)

At 5:10 p.m. the funnel, a half-mile wide, went right across West Boylston Street and up the hill on Burncoat Street into the Greendale section. It was like being at ground zero. The front wall of wind was moving at 300 miles per hour. Four walls are standing in this photograph, but there is nothing inside the house. Other streets stuck in this area were Assumption Avenue, Trottier, Randall, Hyde, Fales, Francis, Fairhaven, and Olin Streets, and Gunnarson Road. (Courtesy of Andrew A. Munter.)

The enormous outward pressure exerted by the relatively high pressure air inside the closed up building bowed the walls outward. Houses were blown into fragments. The power of the wind hammered three-decker buildings into the ground. Some three-deckers caught fire and fell burning on other three-deckers. The wrecking ball had done its work. This woman is sitting on her front stairs a few days later. (Courtesy of Andrew A. Munter)

The tornado struck this area at 5:22 p.m. A couple of walls remain standing on this house. Building after building toppled like dominoes, some just exploded into fragments. Blake Manufacturing of Clinton donated some Ray-O-Vac flashlights to members of Company M. (Courtesy of Andrew A. Munter.)

The tornado struck Main Street in Shrewsbury at 5:22 p.m. on June 9, 1953. Carman Morbidity (left) and Andrew A. Munter are performing a quick search for bodies on Main Street. Houses bulged outward and then burst apart or were just blown off their foundations. (Courtesy of Andrew A. Munter.)

Two cars are demolished among the ruins of these houses in the Greendale section of Worcester, off Burncoat Street. The Guard finally received word from headquarters to pack up and move the unit to Greendale where the funnel had touched down around 5:10 p.m. All they could take was a three-day supply of personnel items, raincoats, blankets, ponchos, and very little money. A series of steel columns can be seen in the picture. The Salvation Army responded quickly with free coffee, donuts, and sandwiches, but the Red Cross charged for their stock. (Courtesy of Andrew A. Munter.)

The tornado slammed into these houses on Main Street in Shrewsbury, ripping off roofs and tearing whole walls away. Only the shell of this house remains standing. Within minutes the area was totally devastated, with walls instantly reduced to splintered lumber, plaster dust, and flying particles of insulation. (Courtesy of Andrew A. Munter.)

Only one utility pole remains standing on the street in the Greendale section of Worcester, off Burncoat Street. The area had no power for a couple of weeks. Many generators could be heard running in the area. In the morning, each guard was assigned a post to stand guard or walk and were provided a challenge and password to keep looters and strangers out of the area. Three days later, a child was found 10 feet off the road in William L. Verdone's vicinity. Anytime something suspicious was observed, guards called their corporal who brought the guard's sergeant in a jeep. Guards either escorted strangers out or brought the police to arrest them. (Courtesy of Andrew A. Munter.)

Wrecked cars were bought to this vacant lot in Great Brook Valley. Looters ransacked the vehicles during the night. (Courtesy of Andrew A. Munter.)

The National Guard arrived in Worcester at about 10:30 p.m. They pitched tents on someone's front lawn and set up security for the area. The next morning, bodies were found inside an overturned car that was crushed by a large tree on a front lawn nearby. Days later, the troops slept on the stage of the Worcester Memorial Auditorium in Lincoln Square. (Courtesy of Andrew A. Munter.)

Several rows of houses were flattened. Some barely remained standing. Leaving the armory, the troops only took a toothbrush and clean underwear for three days. (Courtesy of Andrew A. Munter.)

Officers of Clinton's Company M are having a meeting at their command post. The next detail is getting ready to take their posts on roadblocks. Other streets struck were Crescent, Holden, Lake, Maple, and South Streets, Ireta, Old Mill, Monadnock, and Edgewood Roads, Hapgood Way, and St. James Avenue. (Courtesy of Andrew A. Munter.)

This is the field command post of the headquarters of the 181st Infantry Regiment. Drivers are getting instructions for where they are needed next. Fortunately, the headquarters of the armory was very near where the tornado struck. (Courtesy of Andrew A. Munter.)

On July 4, 1894, a devastating fire struck the downtown area of Hudson. The building where the smoke is coming from is where the fire started. It then burned a great part of Main Street in Hudson. There is one building between the fire and the Washington Street dam. Company M reported for guard duty in the burnt district. (Courtesy of the Hudson Historical Society.)

This view looks up Main Street from Pope Street towards Woods Square where the Hudson fire of July 4, 1894, consumed many of the downtown buildings. Meanwhile, the people of Hudson were at Riverside Park, off Brigham Street, a couple of miles away. Company M reported for guard duty in the burnt district. (Courtesy of the Hudson Historical Society.)

Old Broad's Ford Garage is shown on Washington Street after the 1938 hurricane. MacDonald's is located there now. The large tree is in front of what is now Robinson's Hardware store. The Hudson National Guardsmen of Company L, 3rd Battalion, 181st Infantry Regiment, 26th Yankee Infantry Division were on duty on September 22, 1938. It was an unnamed hurricane that struck southern New England in 1938, causing 600 deaths and 183 mile-per-hour gusts in the Blue Hills of Massachusetts. These are probably Hudson Light and Power linemen cutting limbs off the tree. Linemen wore soft dress hats in those days. (Courtesy of the Hudson Historical Society.)

The location of this large tree, which was uprooted in Hudson during the 1938 hurricane, is in the front yard of a Park Street resident. National Guardsmen of Company L were on duty on September 22, 1938, the morning after the ferocious hurricane, when the town was under martial law. They were on duty primarily to stop looting and keep sightseers away. (Courtesy of the Hudson Historical Society.)

On November 14, 1978, Company B received medals for service during the Blizzard of 1978. Receiving the medals from 1st Lt. John R. Feriero, from left to right, are Pvt2c. Michael J. Parker, SP4c. Vincent A. Chaves, and Sfc. John J. Downing. (Courtesy of Company B.)

Six

AWARDS AND PARADES

In 1956, Company B of Hudson was selected the best of seven tank companies in the 26th Yankee Infantry Division. Capt. Robert J. Rennie received a trophy during field training from assistant division commander Brig. Gen. Otis M. Whitney. Hudson continued to be the best unit in the state, even into the 1990s. (Courtesy of the tank company of the 181st Infantry Regiment.)

These troops stand at attention during the division review at Camp Drum on August 11, 1965. In the foreground on the left is company commander Capt. Harold L. Chapman of Company B. Captain Chapman is about to receive three awards from the governor and division commander. Behind the officers are their guidons. In the third row are the American flags and flags of various battalions. (Courtesy of the tank company of the 181st Infantry Regiment.)

At the division review at Camp Drum on August 11, 1965, Gov. John Volpe presented Captain Chapman with the Armor Leadership Award. He also received the Commanding General Award and the Battalion Commanders Award. (Courtesy of Company B.)

The Grand Army Band is standing in formation on a street in Hudson before the big Hudson fire. From Left to right are George Thompson (leader), William Anton, George Horne, Capt. S. Moore, ? Langdqu, Joseph Leonard, George Eedson, Proctor Pingree, Augustus Trombridge, Herbert Whitney, R. B. Lewis, C. G. Brigham, Charles Ross, George Rand, E. A. Jones, Elliot Ball, ? Fosgate, A. D. Gleason, and Elias Jackson. (Courtesy of the Hudson Historical Society.)

On July 14, 1875, this photograph was taken of the Grand Army Band. The colors, American flag, and regimental flag are on the right. Three companies of the 5th Infantry Regiment, 2nd Brigade, Massachusetts Volunteer Militia are posing in front of town hall in Hudson on an elementary drill on July 14, 1875. Capt. Henry Silas Moore, standing somewhere in front of Company I, had about 24 men at that time. This does not represent a battalion because they did not come into being until 1921. The officers of the regiment are carrying swords and wearing white trousers, while the enlisted men are wearing light blue colors. The only people who carry swords today are the class officers at military academies. (Courtesy of Hudson Historical Society)

Members of Company M are pictured at the armory after their return from the Mexican border on October 27, 1916. During this period, troops were drilled in marching because it involved moving large numbers of troops. The new tactics in this period included having artillery to support infantry and mounted cavalry. The emphasis was for everyone to qualify as an expert with a rifle. With the passing of the National Defense Act of 1916, it gave for the first time major share of the military control to the federal government. The president could now call the state militias (officially designated the National Guard) into service for the full term of their enlistment. This was put to a test when the Guard was called to support the regular army's Mexican border expedition. No guardsmen actually went into Mexico. They spent only four months on this duty. (Courtesy of the Hudson Historical Society.)

This National Guard unit is marching in a Memorial Day parade on May 30, 1947, crossing the Washington Bridge in front of Broad's Ford Garage, presently MacDonald's. After World War II, the unit became an anti-tank company of the 181st Infantry Regiment, 26th Yankee Infantry Division. At the head of the unit is company commander Capt. Emil L. Dion and guidon bearer Joseph Ferrara. The uniform consisted of summer tans, helmet liners, and cartridge belts with first aid packets and .45 caliber pistol side arms. The majorette in front of the band is Janet Rayner. (Courtesy of Joseph W. Lapine.)

In a Veteran's Day parade on November 11, 1951, the heavy mortar company of the 181st Infantry Regiment, 26th Infantry Division, mounted the 4.2-inch mortars in the back of their one-quarter-ton Willy's jeeps. The building to the left is the old counter factory, presently Robinson's Hardware store. The lead jeep driver is Edwin Howe, and the rear driver is Louis Bibi. (Courtesy of Joseph W. Lapine.)

Members of the heavy mortar company of the 181st Infantry Regiment, 26th Infantry Division are pictured during a Veteran's Day parade on November 11, 1951. Not shown in the photograph is the company commander, Capt. James J. Cardoza. On the left is the guidon bearer, George Clayton. In the front row, from left to right, the officers are Levi Lincoln, Melvin Smith, and Herman Oram. Joe Cellucci, Francis Droogan, and James Butland can be identified within the platoon. The uniforms consisted of woolen winter World War II Ike jackets, and helmet liners with YD emblems on the left side. Officers wore pistols, and some senior NCOs carried carbines while the rest of the men carried M1 rifles. A couple of men still wear the old brown boots with the leather buckle at the top. On the right, the men are wearing M1 cartridge belts with plenty of pockets for ammunition clips. Usually, the tank company would have a couple of M47 tanks in the parade, but on hot days the track would tear up the hot top road. (Courtesy of Joseph W. Lapine.)

Both the heavy mortar company in the lead and the tank company following in the line are shown during a Memorial Day parade on May 30, 1952. They are in front of the Hudson Fire Department in Wood's Square. The heavy mortar company would drill on Monday nights and the tank company would drill on Tuesday nights. This year, the division moved the longest motor convoy in military history to Camp Drum. Fourteen trains were used to transport troops. The bus stops in Woods Square and the A&P Supermarket can be seen. (Courtesy of Joseph W. Lapine.)

In 1966, a parade was a scheduled drill, and three full platoons of the company showed up to march. This unit includes an honor guard detail and firing squad. The old parade route in Hudson went from the armory across the Washington Street Bridge, around the rotary circle and down Main Street to Broad Street. It returned to the rotary circle for memorial dedications. The parade stopped at the town hall, the Gold Star Monument, and Veterans Monument at Wood Park.

The color guard of Company B is behind the Veterans Monument at the rotary circle in 1978. Bricks inscribed with the names of veterans have been lined up around the rear of the monument. David R. Marcoux is holding the American flag. (Courtesy of David R. Marcoux.)

At Hudson's centennial parade in June 1966, the commanding officer of Company B was 1st Lt. William L. Verdone. He is followed by guidon bearer S.Sgt. Richard J. Kaloustian. Leading the column of soldiers on the right is 1st Sgt. Anthony M. Kurgan Sr. Directly behind Kurgan is M.Sgt. Donald V. Rutkowski. Leading the column in the center is executive officer 1st Lt. Robert J. Reed. (Courtesy of Hudson Historical Society.)

The *USS Constitution* is turning around for Queen Elizabeth's visit to Boston during Tall Ships day. The mayor of Boston requested that the governor provide support during the scheduled visit of Queen Elizabeth II at the Tall Ships exhibit on August 9 through 11, 1976. The adjutant general then organized a task force to provide civil authorities during this period. The secretary of public safety authorized the use of military forces during this period. Men from the 1st Brigade headquarters were ordered to active state duty and asked to provide communications support to the Boston police and metropolitan district commission police, to protect public safety and property as well as to control vehicle traffic. The task force headquarters was at the police station in District No. 8, on Commercial Street in Boston.

Former State and National Guardsmen from various units met on September 27, 2003, at the Riverside Gun Club on Wilkins Street. The reunion committee, from left to right, included the following: (seated) Armando R. Silva (Berlin), Albert Durand, John Downing, Ronald White (all from Hudson), and Darell Adams (Marlboro); (standing) Jim Collins (Marlboro), Andrew A. Munter (Berlin), Antonio Frias, Ralph Warner, William L. Verdone (all from Hudson), Henry Estabrook (Stow), and Alfred Rio (Hudson). The last reunion of the local company was in 1972, their 25th reunion since the group was federally recognized again in 1947, after World War II. (Courtesy of Rosemary Rimkus, *Hudson Sun* newspaper.)

S.Sgt. Bruce L. Verdone, a member of Troop A, 110th Cavalry Squadron, 26th Yankee Infantry Division, is having a military wedding at the chapel at Fort Devens in September 1990. He was also a platoon sergeant in the honor guard. The Ceremonial Unit includes members of the Massachusetts National Guard. After the bride and groom pass under the arch of sabers, the bride usually gets a slap on the rear with a saber for good luck. Prior to his wedding, Verdone was chosen as the Non-Commissioned Officer of the Year and was awarded a saber. (Courtesy of Brenda Viola.)

At the military wedding in September 1990, the Middlesex County Fife and Drum is providing music for the event. The unit was part of the Massachusetts National Guard Ceremonial Unit, and Verdone's wife, Marla, was a member of the Fife and Drum. (Courtesy of Brenda Viola.)

Harry Fagerquist, a talented, artistic member of the tank company of the 181st Infantry Regiment, 26th Yankee Infantry Division is shown painting a sign, which will hang on the front of the Hudson armory on Washington Street in 1951. Green combat commanders' identification strips were now worn on their uniforms. The armor branch was newly created in the U.S. Army. Armored officers could wear crossed saber emblems. (Courtesy of Joseph W. Lapine.)

This heavy mortar company sign was painted by a Bill Desitel, a professional sign painter on Pope Street behind the Co-Operative Bank in Hudson. The unit was moved to Clinton in 1955, before the sign was finished. It was finished and brought to the Clinton armory by a two-and-a-half-ton truck during a drill. A detail will drill holes in the brick and use rope block and tackle to raise and bolt the sign to the front of the armory. The 4.2-inch mortar is referred to as the regimental commander's artillery. (Courtesy of Darell B. Adams.)

An M60 tank, built in 1959, is pictured with all of its equipment laid out on a canvas. It has a new cupola with a .50-caliber fixed headspace M85 machine gun, a xenon searchlight, a 7.62-caliber NATO ammunition-fixed headspace coaxial machine gun mounted on the turret, and 105-millimeter main gun. Fully loaded, it carries 57 rounds. It can have a bulldozer blade attached, as shown. It has a maximum speed of 30 miles per hour, weighs 51 tons, has a 12-cylinder, V-type, 750 horsepower, air cooled engine, and carries 385 gallons of fuel, a two optical system coincidence range finder, a ballistic computer, and an articulated telescope. The National Guard never received this tank as part of their inventory, but they did receive the M48A5, which had all the modifications. The armor crewmen who trained for six months at Fort Knox were training and firing M60 tanks. (Courtesy of Company B.)

www.ingramcontent.com/pod-product-compliance
Lightning Source LLC
Chambersburg PA
CBHW050635110426
42813CB00007B/1823